Then & Now
Conversations With Old Friends

Then & Now

Conversations

with Old Friends

Edited by Sarah Thursday

Copyright 2015 Sadie Girl Press
ISBN-13: 978-0692549810
ISBN-10: 0692549811
Design and layout by Sarah Thursday
Cover art by Alyssandra Nighswonger
"Looking back into a prism of good and bad decisions and finding
a rainbow–or–Untitled No. 57", 8 x 10 acrylic on wood panel

Edited by Sarah Thursday
Assistant editor Terry Ann Wright
Consulting editor Raquel Reyes-Lopez

SADIE
GIRL
PRESS

Table of Contents

Introduction

Dear Readers,

Like many poets, I began writing as a young teen, full of angst and heartache. My poems began as stolen song lyrics, woven into my own dramatic scenarios. As I matured, my writing matured with me. Recently I realized that while my style of poetry has changed vastly over the years, my subjects have not. I am still writing about heartache with some grown-up angst. As I reread my first poetry chapbook from 1992 (that I literally cut and pasted together), I had this funny idea that if I ever got writer's block, I could always go back and rewrite one of those poems in a modern way. I shared this thought with some other poets and they seemed to think it was a great idea!

Then I thought, wouldn't it be cool to see old and new poems, side-by-side, by a bunch of different poets? We could all see how far we've come as poets over the years. I asked around while presenting at the annual Writer's Weekend at Mt. SAC. Everyone loved the idea. Why not make an anthology of poets and artists showcasing their work from "then" and "now"? Fellow poet K. Andrew Turner suggested the idea of "Conversations with Old Friends" as a title. Each piece would be in "conversation" with the other.

We put out the submission call for pairs of poems and/or art from "Then & Now" and waited for the responses. Many people loved the concept, but interestingly enough, we ended up getting many interpretations of the theme. Some were close to my original idea and others were a different take. They ended up falling roughly into the following four types: 1. a poem written as a young poet paired with a mature version of the same subject, 2. an older poem paired with a revision of the original poem, 3. a poem written at a younger age paired with a direct response or "letter to my younger self" style poem, and finally, 4. two poems written about two different eras in the poet's life.

The art we received also varied from the original theme. In fact, almost all the pairs of images tell a story about the subject of the art as opposed to the artists themselves. Most show a progression of maturity, freedom, and empowerment. Another surprise was the wonderful photos of the poets themselves. They tell their own side of each story, many showing the poets at the age in their "Then" poem.

Each "Then" poem on the left side is preserved in its original submitted state, some with obvious mistakes. Each "Now" poem is on the right side of the page, many of which were actually written just for this project! In the end, this book is more than just about old and new pieces. What you will find is layers of our past selves: the imperfect, the awkward, the ideal, the impulsive, the angry, the naive, and the tragic. It also reveals layers of our present selves: the hopeful, the cynical, the optimistic, the realistic, the strong, the overcoming, and the reflective.

Thank you for picking up this anthology. We hope you will enjoy taking this ride through history, however bumpy it may be!

Warmly,
Sarah Thursday
Editor-in-Chief

Brittni Suzanne Plavala
Age 7, 1997 / Age 24, 2015

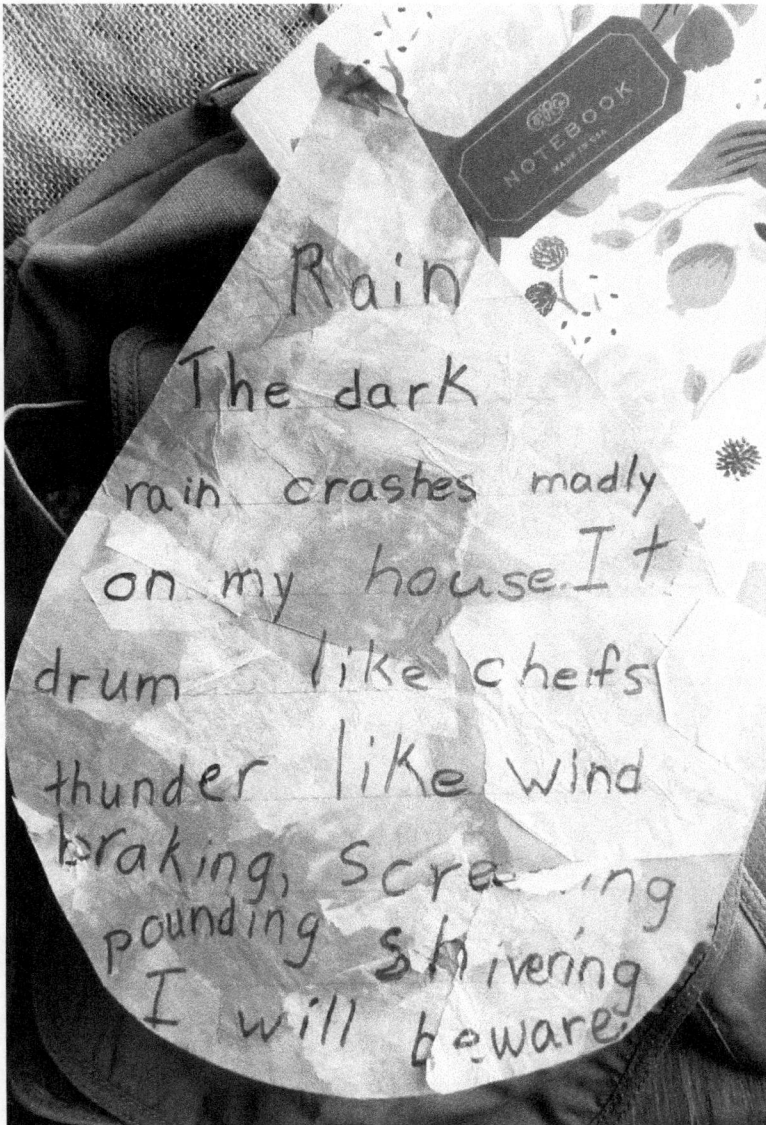

Rain

The dark
rain crashes madly
on my house. It
drum like cheifs
thunder like windos
braking, screaming
pounding shivering
I will beware.

Rainbow

Prismatic arches
pierce the after-storm.
Touching the ground,
triumphant in their stand
like a shaman's chant
breaking the haunt
revealing the truth
answering the quest;
I will be brave.

Myself as a Child

Sharon Elliott
2010/2015

sitting
under the crabapple tree
between the houses
where only harsh punishment
awaited her
for crimes she didn't commit

was like
two worlds colliding
colossal tsunamis
terrible earthquakes
dire landslides slipping down mountains
out of control

she picked up a fallen apple
bitter as the day was long
crunchy
juicy
the perfect size for her small hand

knew
the moment she bit into it
a sour
musty place
became her home

no atonement would save her
no sweet water
bathe her
salty tears

alienation
fed her like vinegar
made from the apples
that nourished her
restitution a wish in the wind
never blowing in her direction

they always asked
how can you eat those apples?
with their dreadful acid taste?

in her wee longing heart
she answered
they are sweeter than your teeth
smaller than a scream
they keep me alive
on a whiff of smoke
in a drafty corner
you can't get to

2

Rose of Sharon
(Hibiscus syriacus)

I am the Roseasharn
lily that survived
dry winds
dirt tornadoes
lived
again

this has nothing
to do with Jesus
the name
belongs to women

if you wear it
stand in power
on calloused feet
only open your arms
to be love
in all its glory
and detritus

remember
the burning times
the crying out loud
the expectations

travel where you will
bring rain
sweet water
salt
and wheat

make bread
in ovens or on hot stones
cover heads with cloth
let tears flow

hide your blade
in the folds of your skirt
the back pocket of your dungarees
behind the hearth

use words
stirred in a bowl
of dust and blood
to sanctify
your roots

K. Andrew Turner
Age 17/Age 30

Fallen For You

Seeing you fills me with giddiness.
Being near you causes me to lose my wit.
I always try to impress you when you are near, have you noticed it?
But I have mixed feeling towards you.
There is the anger for you not noticing me, or do you avoid me?
Arrgh!
And there are the tears I will cry for being alone, without you.
There is joy, pure exhilaration from a word, or a touch,
or even a glance.
I feel my emotions are obvious, perhaps then, you know.
I believe I have just fallen for you.
But, damn! You confuse me so!
I see you acting one way and then another.
The girlfriend, the way you present yourself,
The way you seem to hide, why?
I know we are not buddy-buddy, but you know who I am.
We talk and we have class together.
You have seen me in the halls and the lobby, and you know my name.
People in the hall say it, so why do you avoid or ignore me?
One day we stared at each other.
I know you saw me,
but when I said hello you acted surprised, and embarrassed.
Arrgh!
So why have I fallen for you, my angel?
No clue.

An Open Letter to Ryan Nearhoff

I saw you recently, near
Thanksgiving or Christmas,
walking down the street
in front of my office. I can't recall
who you were with. I remember
seeing your face and going back
in time to when I used to write love poetry
to you. When I asked my friend to give
you the poems I wrote at seventeen.

My stepmom discovered those poems,
knew the secret I'd kept from her and my father.
I had left them in my backpack, and she,
wanting me to have snacks on a flight,
came across those lines I wrote so long ago.

We have changed,
though we never knew each other at all.
My desire, my wanting was more than I could
hold in, pressed with secrets as I was.
And the only thoughts that came to me
were how you could possible like me back—
a bitter lesson about stereotypes I had to learn
again and again and again and again.

I hope you are well. Somewhere,
I saw you were married to her and had a son.
I rarely think of you. But some nights,
in an awful ritual, I research the names of all the men
I've loved who've never loved me back
to see their faces, their lives, and, in nostalgia,
rekindle the feelings so long ago buried
under cold ash that cannot catch.

Steven Marr
Artisit at age 3/Dancing figure as adult

It Will Happen

Every spring the water
becomes fluid again,
breaks into Siberian hunks of ice:
Lake Baikal, 20 million years old,
a thousand unique species,
strange insects lurch to the top,
food for birds; blind fish
with no color scud along the floor.

I reckon 20 million years
warrants my faith.
You will arrive,
have arrived already--
like Rumi's beloved,
you plumb recesses hitherto
explored by naked faith alone.

Clifton Snider
1993/May 2015

It Has Happened

Yes, you arrived
nineteen years ago.
Together we plumbed
the recesses of love and disease
hitherto unexplored,
unanticipated,
dark as a shut garage:
ash from a barbecue
smears the floor,
a noose hangs from the rafter;
ink burns my guts
like a fresh tattoo,
like a poem by Sylvia Plath:
the bleak descent
into insanity or death,
earthquake in Nepal,
avalanche on Everest,
a heap of snow,
a collapse of brick and wood,
body and spirit crushed,
dark as Lake Baikal,
Siberian water
20 million years old; blind fish
with no color scud along the floor.

Love Conditions
for Nancy Aceves

No more pigeons through my window
No more donut-shop crescendo
No more low-life innuendo
I found my voice at last

No more late-night knocking strangers
No more spooky twilight dangers
No more kooky nightlife rangers
I found my home at last

No more girls with piles of trouble
No more trapped inside life's bubble
No more sneaky double double
I found my love at last

Frank Mundo
1998/2015

Love's Condition
for Nancy Mundo

Do us both a favor:
forget our old and tired traditions.
Please don't love me
without conditions.
Challenge me.
Always
expect more from me and of me
always
or don't assume I'll be kind
or always make the right decisions.
Please don't ask for my permission
or put either of us in that position.
Love is editing and revision,
like a poem
always
this poem
always
a first edition.
It only holds value
in mint condition.

Forget those good book phrases
and the ideal good a good world praises.
Challenge me.
Always
make me earn it
always
because doubt is an unfit benefit to give
because you're in the presence of a fool
without exception
without worlds of knowledge
without knowledge of the world.
Life is improvisation and imagination,
like a book
always
this book
always
a signed, first edition.
Its only value
is superstition.

Tripping Over My Machismo

She has nipples like my dad's--
dark circles with erect pencil
erasers--the way they look when
he steps out of the bathroom--
bright with foggy mirrors and bald
light bulb--his hair curled wet
like fish hooks, hot water
beaded on his shoulders, pajama-

pants pulled over his belly-
button--on his way to the living
room to watch TV with Mamá,
until he falls asleep
and she has to wake him
and send him to bed. I wanted
to tell her this while staring
at her nipples, tell her

that I hardly get to see
my dad--except in childhood
memories--and explain to her
how much of a compliment
this observation can be.
I know that she'll take it
the wrong way, button up her
blouse, and tell me to "just leave."

I was willing to risk it,
if only to enlighten
her on my beautiful
discovery. But just when I
mustered the nerve to
articulate my thoughts, she
shoved one nipple into my mouth,
and then something came up.

Overlooking My Machismo

She has nipples like Mama's—
giving way to a chaotic netting of blue
blood vessels—the way I imagine
they looked when she nursed me—
swaddled tightly in that light blue
blanket she knitted with
anticipation—my puffy feat kicking
their way out of the bottom, as she

softly stroked my curls, tenderness
in her eyes that stared beyond my shut
lids—as she imagined what I may grow up
to be, somebody—she hoped—she could
speak proudly of to her *comadres*. I wanted
to tell my wife this while staring at
the suction cup that mouthed her nipple,
as I listened to the heartbeat-like hum

of its motor, and tell that we
are doing fine as young parents—
that everybody struggles juggling
work and family—that Mama managed
without language or much money.
I know she'll appreciate—despite the soreness
and dwindling drips—and eventually welcome
the unsolicited advice that "it gets better."

I wanted to comfort her with
my knowledge of a mother's bond—
something I will never know,
and secretly resent—
but she's known it for months—
established before he was even born—and
I witness it every time she holds him
in her arms, knowing she'll never let him down.

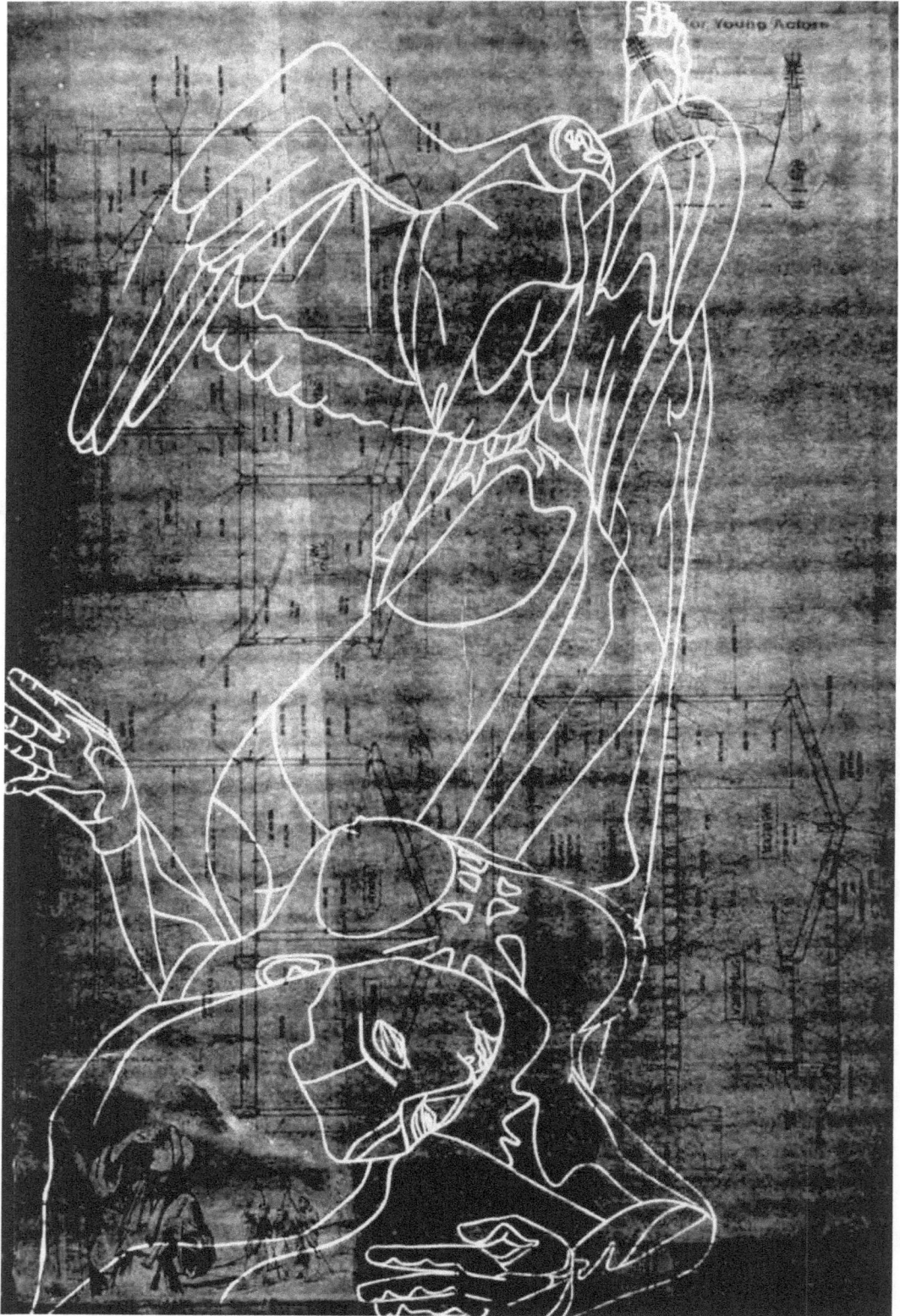

Joy Shannon
Blueprint vulture/Leda

The Days

After your birdsong departure, I tiptoe
down the carpeted hall, breathe the steam
your showered body has left. Even though

the kids are grown, the same train whistles
you away to fight in that bank language
I can't stand, learned from your father's

dull school— for the sake of financing
this fantasy— the one we've passed
to our sons and daughters— you know it's lonely

inside this hollow palace when you're away
too long. To survive the hours I shop for dresses,
and silky chocolate. But I always come home

when the train whistle blows and the sun glows low
to drink in the swills of your perplexing adoration—
my obstinate dream.

Carla Carlson
Father's Day 2003/Father's Day 2015

To the Father of My Children

You dear, riveted my soul
some thirty years ago—yes
then, you were always the father of my children,
as when you were a small boy with combed hair,
taking orders from sisters in the Mormon home,
even then you were the father of my children.
And when you were a devilish—dangerous boy
smoking with fellow dwellers of the church's attic,
or crawling through the underworld, the under-town—
via sewers, like a marine, like a man seeking, you
already knew you were the father of my children—
didn't you? Faring forward, leading others, at 21—
wearing your giant beating heart first, (formidable!)
for lights on unsafe paths, lighting the paths, you
must have known by then you were the father of
my children. The night I met you, I knew, before
one in-breath—you had always been
the father of my children.

Gerald Locklin
Age 20/Age 74

Route 36

I go back in search of summer
      Phillipsburg, Kansas five-buck motel
Where mosquitoes suffocated
    And the lull of wheat was terrible
In Phillipsburg, Kansas
   (And the carny was in town)
My child bride wept because
    The miles washed by
        Without a word
   As reticent as rain
I sought in vain
            The center of the continent
Opening of the field
Where wheat is summer
And winter ripe against the open sky

With sadness in my hands and face
    Because my child bride wept
Because the miles went by

Thumbnail Guide for the Senior Couplers

No matter how you coupled,
if you coupled at all,
and if it was fun while you were doing it,
and you came (or close) at the end of it,
who cares who was putting what into whom,
where, or how many times?

These and many other details are INESSENTIAL!!!
Maybe it was just a damn fine back rub!!!
It's not even ESSENTIAL that there be a next time,
it's more ESSENTIAL that you retain a memory
OF THIS TIME . . . and even a SENSE MEMORY
OF SOMETHING HAVING HAPPENED
will suffice.

As far as the next time is concerned,
well, you've earned a next time,
but then again, we don't always get to cash
our final pension checks either.

And, anyway, was there ever a time in our lives
when, man or woman,
LGBT or straight, we knew for sure
where our next piece of ass was coming from,
OR even IF one was? And, as anyone will tell you:
the worst piece of ass you ever had
was probably not all THAT BAD either!
And who knows, maybe we take our memories with us,
except up there, they're not just dreams, they're
like a porno film in which we star eternally,
and God's a smiling, ageless popcorn-popping
pharmacist, distributing these little blue pills.

Erica Brenes
2005/2013

Dirty Kisses

III.

When I kissed you that first time, it felt like watching home videos
that hadn't been recorded yet.

It was that big of a deal.

I remember driving you home afterward. You turned the radio off,
looked me straight in the eyes and asked with a type of sexy
presumption that you wore like your father's oversized blazer,
"Erica, be my girlfriend." And I closed my mouth and tried to shake
you, tried to shake the memory of our mouths combining. Tried to
pretend that I hadn't seen what I saw, felt what I felt. You kissed
me and the tape started rolling, the clock started ticking. I had
wanted so many things, but you kissed me and everything changed.
I threw out my old map, and I said, "Sure, let's call today our
anniversary." Your mouth, your silly, funny, quirky, mouth. Suddenly
I wanted you, to please you, to be everything you wanted me to be,
everything you were asking me to be. When we kissed that night, with
my legs folded neatly beneath me, with our hands in our own laps, you
pushed me, and I tumbled. Tripping like Alice, head first into the
abyss of my future, dragging you right behind me- into a rabbit hole
you and I both weren't necessarily ready for, but with closed eyes
and a happy mouth, I kissed you back.

Sharing something underground, mouthing passwords indiscreet, with
tongues tied, we hushed our closeted lists of expectations, our long
lists of fears and anxieties, and when we started to get excited, and
our bodies quickened and we accidentally bumped our teeth into one
another, I giggled because I wanted to misstep with you, be confused
and slip up with you. I wanted to build a life around you, swap your
burdens for mine, sign Christmas cards with a shared last name. I
wanted Sundays with you and Monday through Saturday too. Tangled
like virgin teenagers hopped up on broken curfews and cold pizza, we
kissed and I decided on you.

Dirty Kisses

III.

At our wedding, Barry White crooned, "My First, My Last, My Everything" while I kissed a little piece of your neck that hid beneath your white collar and your checkered tie. My body seldom feels right to me, seldom belongs, but right then, in that moment, I was where I needed to be. With my strong hand nesting in your left, our hip bones pressed together like book ends, that evening, you invited me home.

And since then, all it ever takes is the smallest amount of contact. Mouth to mouth, finger tips to finger tips, my palm curved up around your shoulder, thumb to clavicle as we dance on the hard wood floors in our dining room, or sometimes, and this is my favorite, my lips on your forehead as you sleep, breathing evenly while I grade late into the night, or my mouth, slightly open against the inside of your palm, breathing you in and kissing out softly, as we watch movies side by side, or perhaps even my mouth against your bearded cheek as you leave for work and I drink coffee in front of an open lap top.

That's all it takes, and I am home again.

Once I Met a Buddha

Once I met a Buddha
Traipsing down the hall
Chatting with the principal
Standing proud and tall
I watched her holy procedures
Scheming to cut science class
And then, with amazement,
I found it was me
Just my reflection in a chemistry glass.

Avra Kouffman
Age 11, 1977/2005

The Goddess of Breathing

Can you articulate the essence of an article of faith?
I think I can. It's akin to admitting
five senses don't grasp everything.

Sometimes you get an inkling—there's something more
outside. A flicker here—a flutter there—

The ear of the spirit can hear it.
The soul of the spirit can hold it.

Not forever; the way you hold a breath
for as long as you need
to keep breathing

Hearts quicken;
day-to-day, our minds forget.
Til God comes sweeping
through a laugh, a breath

& this inspires you to stave off death
Take as long as you need,
to keep breathing

Sarah Lim
Kitchen 2005/SOL Kitchen Goddess 2013

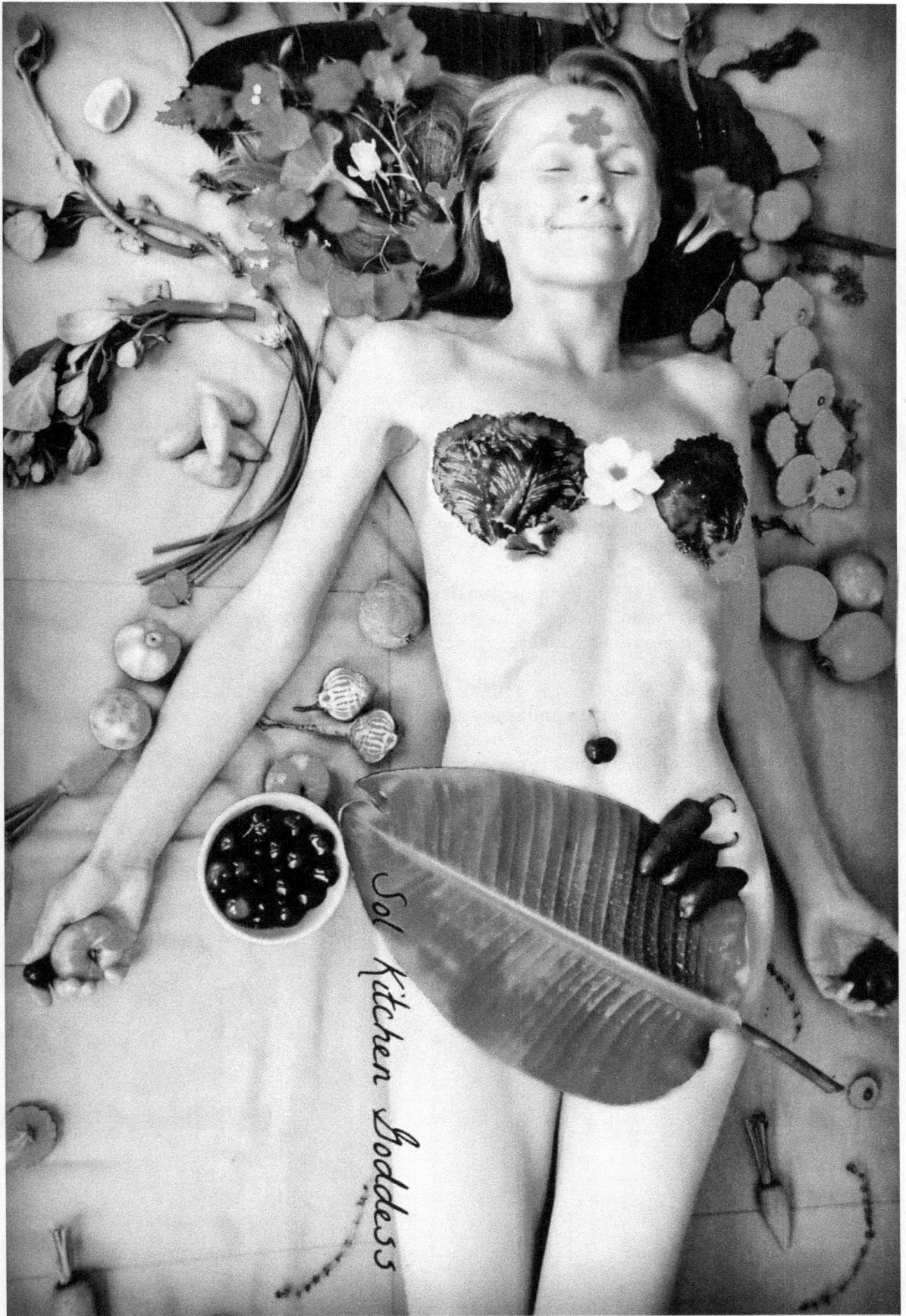

Sol Kitchen Goddess

Grandma's Kitchen

I want to taste my grandmother's kreplach.
She pounded, kneaded then rolled the dough,
cotton towel covered the soft ball
as it rested on her white enamel stove.
She chopped onion, beef, then finally fried--
standing barefoot on those plump Polish feet.
Apron tied tight around a wonton waist.
Gold facet hoops swung fast as she saw my face.
And that wiry white hair against her brown eyes—
like mine, but far more lined than fine linen.

It was not the kreplach creation I would.
watch in awe. It was just Leah. The old woman
once shy young girl at Ellis Island, alone and only
sixteen. Same girl in my photo at Coney. Again
barefoot, firmly planted in the Brooklyn sand.

I do miss my grandmother's kreplach soup.
Those heavy dumplings floating in fat,
simmered in the pot so we could stroll
on Brighton's boardwalk passing her old men.
They would wave and yell, "Leah!" but no luck.
She never stopped—surely no sweet thing.

I want to taste grandma's kreplach again.
To see her standing so serious by the stove
ladling hot soup to me and my dad--
to be in Brooklyn—to be their sweet girl.

Julie Standig
2009/2014

Grandma's Kitchen

I met Leah when I was nine. She sat behind
at my brother's Bar Mitzvah.
Who's that funny looking lady?
Your grandma. My mom.

Her Brighton Beach apartment uniquely hers:
thick metal bar that locked floor to door.
Plaster foot with geraniums on top.
Is that Hebrew on the stores? No. Russian.

But she was from Warsaw
before the war
before the others saw.

Mostly I remember her kitchen, the window
that overlooked rooftop, the elevated
subway, which rattled the venetian blinds
every time the B whizzed by.

White wallpaper looked like bricks
with green ivy crawling—pointing
to one direction
the kitchen's corner.
A mannequin stood alone.

Short and squat like Leah. Same broad
bust, waist, hips.
A skirt or shirt always pinned in place.
Leah, proud card member of LGWU.

Once she measured me for a wool jumper.
Tape, pins, fabric and her hands all over me.
Must have made it on the mannequin—
it was as big as my disappointment.

Nothing legal about Leah:
perhaps it was the bathtub gin
or card games with Dutch Schultz.
Maybe the pajamas, umbrellas and blouses
sold direct from her closet.

But I miss this woman I never got to know.
I miss the smell of simmering soup,
the flash from her gold facet earrings,
and her hands that held her hips, that held off
the old men who called her name.

West Andover

At three in the morning,
Great buckets of rain.
On the road - dark drops
And then a flood.
Rippling sheets of water move the leaves
Against the brush,
Along the poison ivy.

A woman with her dreams
Rolls over in her bed.
What was it that she wanted long ago
As she walked the grassy field behind the house
And in the sunlight felt so free?

Beneath the canopy of trees,
Where once her father walked and held her hand,
The well worn path around the pond turns black.

Words for Rain

what name for a mist in early summer
that thickened on the canopy of pine
till droplets fell to darken and dapple
the paths which led around the pond
to the place we called Perch Cove

rain as verb   to lavish or bestow
great buckets of rain   so sudden
they absolve the layers of festering dust
that on a damp mid-summer night
break loose the clots of memory

what name for the driving lashing rain
that splattered on the windshield glass
in ever-changing circles and rivulets
and dodged the syncopated wipers
for one hundred turnpike miles

and what name will finally satisfy
the weeks of late September rain
cold against your upstairs window
disquieting the inner cracks
threatening to freeze and split the soul

Esmeralda Villalobos
Self portrait, age 4/Self portrait, 2013

ESMERALDA V.

Boris Ingles
2010/2015

9 windows 4 tellers

In a seller
with 20 faithful line dwellers.
Grunting,
sighing,
hanging,
in single file
one foot at a time.
Wondering why on earth
do they have 9 windows and 4 fucking tellers?
fuck!
My lunch is on its half
and you 4 are a hand-job away from
blowing my mind.
But who am I
to hiss,
grunt,
and hang?
I'm just a faithful line dweller
who needs his check cashed.
whatever
I should've gotten direct deposit.

nine windows & four tellers

we piss & moan
along the edge

filing slowly
in & out of debt
one measured foot
at a time

we speak softly
like crazies
in soup kitchens

grunting our wrath
as we coil slowly
through this
regurgitated
waste

we wait & wait
for these four mopes
to bang us
out of loot

to haggle
for our soul

to guide us
through this
regurgitated
waste

maybe
i'm being sour
a little erratic
after all

i'm still
the only mope
without direct deposit

Load Bearing

I wanted to call out to you
as you loaded up your back seat
with everything you had left
over the years,
but your name sank into my torso
and settled in my gut.

It filled my stomach with cement
and constructed a cathedral to rest in
that displaced my diaphragm,
and forced my lungs against my ribs.
The finishing touch was a spire
that shot through my esophagus
to scrape the back of my throat.

I've since taken toothbrush handles
to purge your name from my body,
but all I can get out is the clack
of plastic on stone
that echoes down through the lonely church
where your name remains encased
in a shrine can't be removed.

Brandon Dumais
Winter 2013/Spring 2015

34

Country Boy

I scream along to Phosphorescent's
"Joe Tex, These Taming Blues Are Killing Me"
driving home from work
at night, my crackled rasp
over the pubescent whine from the stereo,
both struggling to maintain the notes
in "ain't you still sweet to me?"

I recall reading Leee Childers describe
meeting Sid Vicious for the first time,
finding the punk poster boy crying alone
to Jim Reeves, and sitting and crying with him.

I recall my grandmother singing along
to Tammy Wynette and Hank Williams
in her heavy Indonesian accent
while my parents were away,
years before she died.

I recall myself as a child,
the incredulity in every adult
as they remarked on how "bright"
and "mature" I was for my age,
my disdain for childish things
that kept me from truly outgrowing them.

I remember Kate,
her fondness for cartoons,
her sprightly affection
that stripped the veneer of adulthood
from my skin and shot
childhood back into my veins,
her warm body I explored
like a boy in a sun-kissed wood,
roaming deeper to the call
of her nascent moans.

I remember her in every good country song I hear,
every languid note of the slide,
every buzz and twang and hum.
And I yearn and seethe
out of angst and self-loathing,
like a child who doesn't want to be one
anymore.

Ken Oddist Jones
This is not an exit/Exit

D'où Venons Nous/Que Sommes Nous/Où Allons Nous
Where do we come from/What are we/Where are we going

The spring after my divorce was final
you took me to the MFA. Do you
remember? Still a wintry April, but
it was Mary Cassatt that month, and you
had tickets. White petals dropped from blackened
branches, snow banked against the museum
walls, and we disembarked from the E train.
Mary hummed in muted orange and gold.
Before we left we wandered through other
halls, other rooms, coming to rest in front
of Gauguin. Bodies floated among trees, a
cool blue Buddha peered out. You told me the
story you saw there. I countered with my own,
our arms outstretched as if to warm our hands.

Terry Ann Wright
2000/2015

D'où Venons Nous/Que Sommes Nous/Où Allons Nous
Where do we come from/What are we/Where are we going

Two years and seven months after you died
your mother sends me a box of your books.
(Your library: lovingly collected, curated,
a stand-in for you: passionate, beautiful.)
When they arrive, I tear into the carton
in the post office parking lot. Foamy
packing peanuts blow in the breeze.
It is not what I expect. Only a pile of books,
plunked into a garbage bag, haphazard:
a yellowing paperback resting against
The Mouse of Amherst. One last surprise:
the smell of cigarette smoke is so strong
I have to cram the box in my trunk.
You are not there. You are not anywhere.

Robin Steere Axworthy
2005/2015

Mother

Mother,
moon,

darkness and brown red flesh
            I inherit
cannot be subject to.

If
you could have told me,
            growing up,
cries are sometimes joy,
that love is only made
            in secret places,
dark inheritance;
that tearing pain
and bleeding,
            my brother's birth:
darkness breaks
            to mucous
                    blinking
                    light.

        But how could I know?

Mother,
your strength overwhelms me.
your grandmother,
my great grandmother,
you mother,
me, your granddaughters,
flame and lengthen
into once dark well,
holding stars and moon,

mind and spirit sunk
into its source
and washed in night

I wish sometimes
        I were
                the sun.

Mother 2

"Leave me alone!" she says,
"Or just kill me now."
She means that she sees no point
in moving, in getting up.
It is too much to think of dressing,
of eating, of another day.

Her dreams claim her, she says,
wiggling through her brain
like worms through jello.
Now is not a now she recognizes.

Later she gets up;
we help her to the commode,
and wipe her bottom,
still broad with our births,
with carrying us and pushing us
out into this world.

We help her dress. She will sit
doing the crossword puzzle
in pen, and reading and rereading
the comics, explaining the jokes once,
then again if we ask why she laughs.

How is it that she is still she, she wonders.
She says, "I wonder about the meaning of life."
She means that she cannot do the way she once did:
cooking, cleaning, cuddling, caring.

I say, "You spent your life doing.
Let us take care of you now."
I mean that her love still holds us,
a firm circumference girdling each of us
each day, while her days fade like mist,
like smoke, her life a fire
to which she gave herself;
we gather each ember, husbanding
its shape, its warmth, this fire,
to light us into the dark.

Neverland

There he is, that's my father
I used to miss him
but now I know who he is
He's just like those newspaper stories
we thought were so important
but now they're just trash
Just the same as all those love letters
from my former lovers
who didn't know who I am
so I sit with the lies of my father
the prayers of my mother
and your heart in my hand
if it ends, will you jump with me?
hand in hand
just like we were Peter Pan and Wendy
off to Neverland
where it makes more sense
then these lies and their governments
the tension in these strings
its scares me just like the dark
or the thought of you turned to him
breaking my heart
these thoughts keep me awake
of wars for no reasons at all
or meaningless of losing you to a bar brawl
I swear the songs keep closer to heaven every time
all the writers of babel keep adding their own
while the rest of the world sinks closer to hell
we're just writing songs to make this feel like home
maybe it will come true
just like the bible is to you
but tell me will you remember me when
you and me
we were Peter Pan and Wendy
off to Neverland
and we lived all the songs we write
we live forever in just one night

Joy Shannon
2007/2015

Tir na nÓg

I was once in Tir na nÓg
And now it lives in the whispering words from my heart
And the glimmers of music echoing through the halls of my thoughts
This is what compels me to pluck strings and sing its reflection
Every painting first began as a memory of the divine
Every song is a haunted memory of who I once was
Like smoke through the blood of who I am

My ancestors are still with me
with every rise and fall of my chest
Their drums beat my heart on
I know why I came back
with my head held high
Even though carrying deep sorrow
with a foot in both spirit and earthly worlds
I shed the darkness to make room for more light
Every day I sing and they sing in my bones
When I stand in my power
They clap their hands
Only I hear
but sometimes the lights flicker
just to make sure I remember they are there.

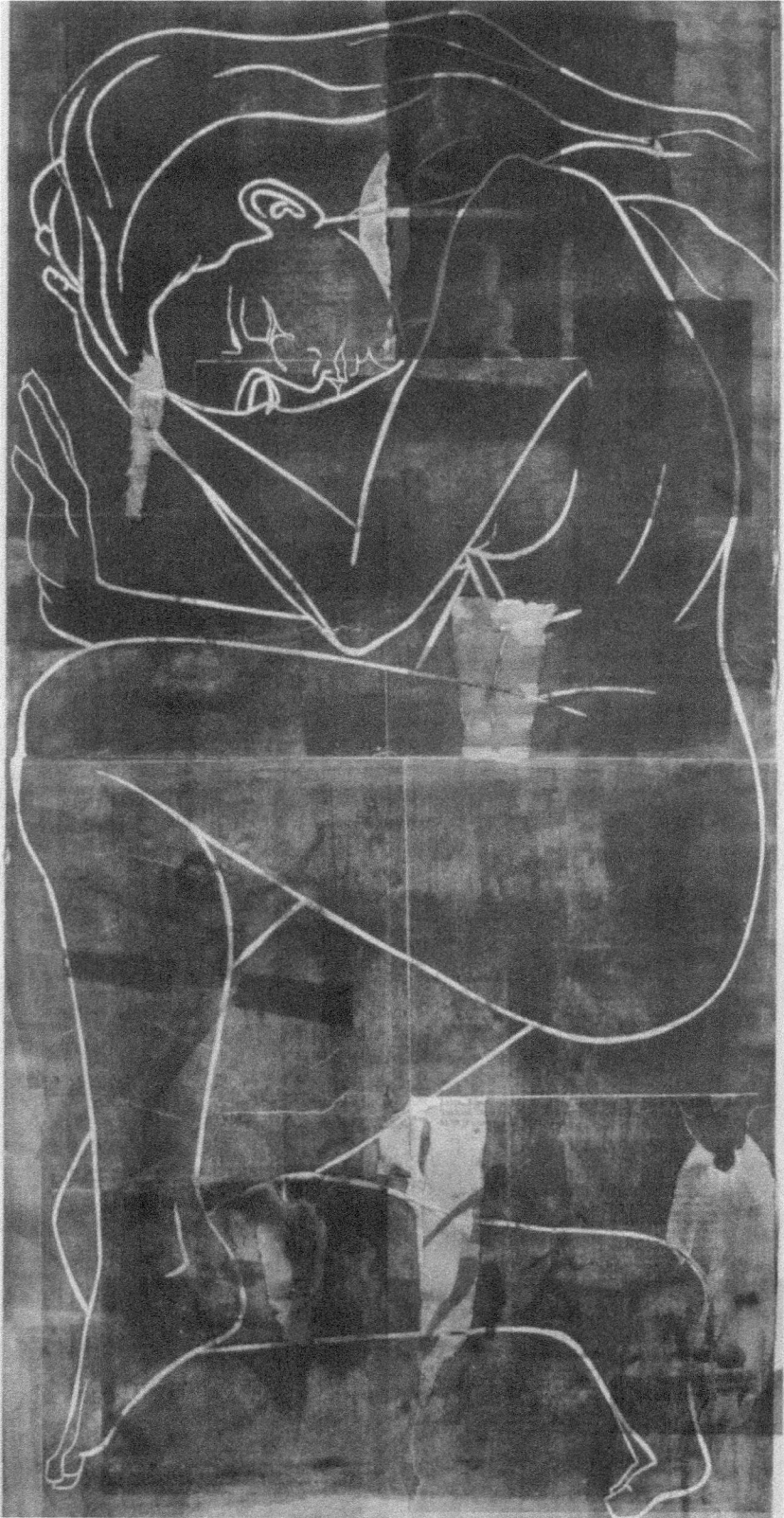

Joy Shannon
Woman contained #2/ Mnemosyne

To The Grandfather I Drove To The Pines

I blame life, life and all its clockwork
    For stealing you, and changing you
    Until you resembled nothing so much
    As that game of solitaire we played,
        One card missing, almost normal.

Almost normal, except for that time in the rain
    When your joints locked up, your mind
    Locked down, and you stood there on the steps,
        Frozen like the tiny fish trough in December,
        Little goldfish darting underneath the
                Thin ceiling of ice.
You were holding one foot in the air and both hands on the rails,
    Shaking without a jacket, and me slipping
    As I tried to get under you, tried to push
    Your foot back down, just a little farther.
        "Come on, grandpa. Just a few more steps."

And I remember standing beside you as a boy of eight,
    When you signed the papers and smiled sadly,
    Chief Joseph tears in your eyes as you waved
    Goodbye to your frail mother, her mind scattered
    Like debris after an accident on the highway
                But her eyes
    Her eyes staring into yours with blue intensity
    And her chicken-thin arms wrapped around your own
    While you hung your head and admitted her
              To The Pines.

You left with that Marine discipline that sustained you all your life
    And you made everyone swear to you, swear to you
    That no matter what, they would never do to you
           What you just did to her.

You made them all promise, except for me, because I was too young.
    They kept their promise, Grandpa, but life never
    Yields to our demands, and it's probably for the best
    And a million other clichés that ring like the bell
    At a boxing exhibition. Ding. Round twelve, over.
           But they kept their promise, Grandpa.

Did she forgive you? Do you forgive me? Does time
    Know the pain it's caused to one who can't remember
    His own name, tie his own shoes, or walk a straight line?
          Does it at least have the mercy
              To let you forget?

Brandon Williams
2006/2012

Celadon

My grandmother sat on a gray-green couch holding a red plastic cup of vodka and lectured me on grammar. "You do not *continue on*," she told me. "*Continue* and *on* are redundant. Excise the unnecessary." She sipped and grimaced, and a touch of the silver liquid fell off the edge of her lip. I watched it land on the couch and continue on, rolling over and into the gray-brown carpet near my Lionel train set. I was seven years old. The conductor's face, riding staunchly aboard the lead engine, was a stiffly painted-on smile.

Today, I pull an old gray-green plate from her cupboard. I cover the plate with two pieces of wheat bread, make a sandwich with peanut and apple butter, both canned in this kitchen. The house smells of eucalyptus. She's lying in bed. I can hear her soft moans of discomfort. The diagnosis came out of the blue. I'm afraid she's given up. The doctor said, "For quality of life, there's not much to be done." The doctor said, "Expect broken bones. It's in the marrow." The lamp light is gray-yellow. When I bring her sandwich and medication, my face is a stiffly painted-on smile. There's no comfort I can offer. Her bedspread is gray-tan. Every color I see is a variation on that celadon couch where I learned that I could continue, or I could go on, but I couldn't do both.

Steven Marr
Dancing figure #3/Dancing figures

Brian Christopher Jaime
1991/2015

Hope Never Dies

The old woman sat by the window waiting for her son to come home
from World War II. She began to remember about all the times
they had spent together—Christmas, Easter, Thanksgiving. Oh,
Thanksgiving—they used to feast on pies and turkey. She smiled
as the beams of sunlight reflected against her wrinkles. Old and
weary, she stood up with her hand over her eyes to block the rays
of sunlight. She smiled and looked out the window. Her grin faded
as she sat back down. Her son was late as usual. A knock at the
door brought her to her feet; it was her son, he was home. The door
opened—
"Hello Mrs. Potts, how are you?" said a man who was dressed all in
white. Her son looked handsome she thought.
"Johnny, what day is it?"
The man stared.
"The date? Is the war over? Can you finally stay home for good?"
"It's October twenty-third," the nurse replied. "Nineteen ninety."
Confused, she sat back down and looked out the window again.

Gone

I went to your house today. You remembered I was coming. And to take a bath. And eat. You told me a story that happened yesterday, not seventy-five years ago. You didn't ask the same question thirteen times. There was no argument about prescription drugs or bloodwork. You didn't slam the door. But, of course, none of that happened. How could it? You are here and you are gone.

Cattle Train to Magdeburg

My mother still remembers

The long train to Magdeburg
the box cars
bleached gray
by Baltic winters

The rivers and the cities
she had never seen before
and would never see again:
the sacred Vistula
the smoke haunted ruins of Warsaw
the Warta, where horse flesh
met steel and fell

The leather fists
of pale boys
boys her own age
perhaps seventeen
perhaps nineteen
but different
convinced of their godhood
by the cross they wore
different from the one
she knew in Lvov

The long twilight journey
to Magdeburg
four days that became six years
six years that became sixty

And always a train of box cars
bleached to Baltic gray.

My Mother Reads My Poem
"Cattle Train to Magdeburg"

She looks at me and says,
"That's not how it was.
I couldn't see anything
except when they stopped
the boxcars and opened the doors

And I didn't see
any of those rivers,
and if I did, I didn't know
their names. No one said,
'Look, look this river
is the Warta, and there
that's the Vistula.'

What I remember
is the bodies being
pushed out—sometimes
women would kick them out
with their feet.

Now it sounds terrible.

You think we were bad women
but we weren't. We were girls
taken from homes, alone.
Some had seen terrible things
done to their families.

Even though you're a grown man
and a teacher, we saw things
I don't want to tell you about."

John Guzlowski
1978/2003

She holds a metal rod
over the earth

She's learned to meditate
to not tremble
to lightly walk with
the weight of her children
and the image of planes
dropping bombs over
her village many years ago

Her breath is
light
like the rhythm
of vivaldi's four seasons
her heart keeps
a steady beat

The beeping detecting
an unexploded bomb
makes her pause
but she is strangely calm
though the sun is too hot
and it is humid
and the beeping mixes
with her heartbeats

There is not a posture
more beautiful than
when she kneels down
with her shovel
and gently
carefully digs

knowing that each
movement of the
shovel could
cause the bomb
to explode

and her life

would end like
so many others
during the war
and after the war
so unexpectedly

or perhaps
she will be
lucky and only
lose part of her
body - an arm
or leg

she has learned
to identify each
type of bomb
the way some
learn the name
of flowers
and animals

when she finds
the bomb
she stops digging
and places a marker
at the site

and she is filled
with joy
her smile widens
wide as the farmer's field
and the laughter of children
running through fields

The Gambler

The metal rod she holds is her wand
the deck is more than 52 cards
her suits: bombs used on both sides of the war -
M14, đap lôi, mìn muôi
she walks in the wild fields seeking the invisible
bringing it to the surface in a strange beauty
of smoke and explosion
the wager is her life or a limb
the shovel, a tongue that lifts the crumbling earth
to reach an unexploded landmine
she spreads out the dirt beneath her hands like cards

Freedom

In my youth I dreamed
of things not yet'
longing for the
supposed sweet taste.
I'd while away the hours
planning, wondering what
it would be like. Thoughts
of great things to do and see
crashed upon my reality
like the waves at sea.
Always in awe of the
magical mystery.
I could not wait. It
seemed such a long time
coming. And then suddenly,
mysteriously even, I found myself,
a MAN

The world opened tp me
like to a summer storm.
My own energies and directions
the only limits.
Bursting across the horizon,
or painstakingly cautions,
I set my own pace.
Opening all doors, or none at all.
Life is my gift,
the living of it mine!
Free—Freedom!!!

Kevin Patrick Sullivan
1982/2015

Freedom

I'm not as young as I used to be
Bob Dylan said I'm older than that now
What does it mean to be free?
A free man in America
It depends on your color
Nina Simone said freedom is the lack of fear
Malcolm X said question authority
I try to live without fear
To question authority
It has been made easier by the
White skin I was born in
I thank god for that
Otherwise I'd probably be dead
When I was in my early twenties
Six of us riding around in a car
Smoking pot drinking beer
We were pulled over by the Michigan State Police
They took our driver's licenses and were running them
I had to pee—so yeah I opened the door
Ran out into the night
For the closest tree
Halfway there I was told to stop or he would shoot
He had pulled his gun—he was in a shooter's stance
I said go ahead but I've got to pee
If I was a black man someone else'd be talking to you now

Another Fourth of July...

another time for ravish and carnage -
no time for the atheist's bliss.

On the outskirts, no time for Aristotle.

We're just in time for nightsweats and quarantine,
just in time for blackmail and burlesque.

Grandfather's clock is naïve in Pennsylvania, in India,
and we're all Midwestern miniatures.

This isn't 1890, time of a terrible cocoon -
this is a time of slaughter & soliloquy
             of impending & anonymous.

Where is the hunch of fireboats?
Aren't there zippers in the firmament?

I feel all kindling and epilogue,
             all vagabond and scaffold,
                 all ornament...

as a country, we are medieval, addict, November -

gone the time of trajectory, of leopard,
gone the time of lexicon, gone the granite.

We stand beneath umbrellas in a thicket
             with coins for utensils,
                 an irregularity in the navy;

but this is no time to be courteous!

Call the church-going secretaries! -
pay any price for their radium.

This is a time for bark and lantern,
             for chafe and shaft,
to remove the tin from the trapdoors.

Let the custodians dazzle
with their sorcery,
find the fissure in the swamp,
interrupt.

Leave the distended asylum -
this is the time for hormones.

Lynne Thompson
1990s/2014

Another Fourth of July,

another year of ravish, carnage.
No time for bliss.

No time for Benjy Franklin's kites.

Just enough time for night-sweats &
quarantine, murder, then the fiddling.

This isn't the nineteenth century—
that time of our terrible cocoon.

This is a time of slaughter, of coin as utensil,

and we blacks feel like kindling, epilogue
in a country that's medieval and often, cruel.

Gone the times of the forefathers' inventions
carved into our monumental granite,

sewn into our courteous flags.

This is the time for bark and shaft, time
to remove the trap from trapdoors,

time to dazzle with our sorcery and then
challenge and defy when we must.

Judy Barrat
March 1959/March 2015

Seeking the Light

I wandered down a darkened path
A light glowed at its end
I was alone and so afraid
But the light - it was my friend.
Frantically I made my way
through the darkness so like night
Past shadows of familiar things
to reach that friendly light.
The strangest thing occurred just then:
As I approached the glow,
The nearer that I came to it,
The more faint did it grow.
When at last I reached the place
Where my friendly light did shine
I saw a blurred reflection
which to my distress was mine
I looked into the glass again
And sorrow filled my heart
For the light I sought so desperately
was way back at the start!

The Road

I left behind the street of childhood
to navigate the highway of life,
exchanged dirt of backyard and joy of
sandbox for dust of the open road.
In a haze of youthful exuberance, I
searched for adventure described in books.
I climbed mountains, crossed deserts,
sailed seas to cities and streets in lands
far and near; encountered life, both sweet
and simple, and shockingly brutal and
barbaric and stood impotent, in my naïveté
to do more than extend a hand. And some-
times, only sometimes, it was enough.
I found joy and generosity in places of dire
need and deprivation, sadness and
selfishness in the midst opulence and plenty.
No longer do I walk carefree, inhaling
nature's bounty, but run, frantic, in an
endless quest for—HOME, as I mourn
the death of innocence and damn the
dawn of disillusion. On this narrow track
of time every now becomes then in
the blur of contemplation of tomorrow.
And while each impediment in this path
may proclaim: this Road Leads Nowhere,
I find the fortune I believed this trip would
provide when I or anyone extends a hand.
For me, that is enough.

Alexis Rhone Fancher
Zoe at age 14/Zoe at age 16

She, Angel

She drinks from pictures
of angels on the sides of a clean
mug pressed to her lips

She lies down later on
next to my decrepit body,
pieces of flesh rotting between
the sheets of my bed,
my eyelids collapsing over my pupil.

She doesn't let me sleep.
Her smile is far too bright,
her touch grafts skin over
my leprosy,
her voice quells banshees
swimming in my ear,
holding their heads underwater.

She doesn't notice her wings
stretching across the room,
sewing together hope
shredded by my illness,
singing sweet choruses,
seducing sorrow away from my eyes

She doesn't notice I smile
as she takes me into the sky

Marcus Clayton
2012/2015

She, Angel

She wakes me. My knees grip ground,
    feathers cradle the circumference,
      two flesh wounds gape
      where my shoulder blades
      fell off. Red lines string
        string down my back—
        a bloodied Nile—the jaundice
        holds my skin like a scared
        baby clung to a mother's blouse
          crying as I cry.

She stands in front of stars with light
    collapsed over her head, black tarp
    of sky behind like a proud parent,
      her hand a marble white
with polished fingers that reach
for my splintered ones,
          my limbs of dry rot, the yellow
    that aches the hair on my arms

She catches the bile from my mouth
    but the stench does not glove her,
    assures, "it'll be ok," and her voice
    quells the banshees that swim
    inside my ear, and she sews
      the feathers onto lesions,
        but I still cannot fly.

She catches my crumbled carcass,
    her plumage sprouts 10 feet
    each direction. I feel
my knees breathe and my toes
lose grip of gravel. The moon
is out and washes my jaundice,
    her marble, in blue.

She makes the moon bigger, smile
    wide as her wingspan.
    Oceans crash below
us. This must be death,
but I do not care.

Suzanne Allen
1985/2015

Date Night

A call on the phone - he'll meet her at eight.
Her heart skips a beat as she stands by the gate.

He opens the door and she steps inside.
The feelings between them are too strong to hide.

They drive in the dark on a moonlit night.
He pulls to the side, and they talk of the fight.

"It was awful," she says. "I missed you a lot."
"I can't live without you. We shouldn't have fought."

A kiss mends it all for those who've found love.
Then their dreams travel on like an innocent dove.

Postcard to Pat Regarding the Movie *Valley Girl*

You were neither my first love, nor my last, but that summer evening by the wave pool, for once, I did not even care about the lifeguards. It was all so fourteen and pointless. Boy crazy and wanting trouble, I found your eyes clear and bright; now that I think about it, they were the color of mine, how you looked into me like Randy might, that punk-rock prince from the wrong side of town. After that I was always looking for you, but you were almost never there. I wanted to tell you that movie was made for us. I still own it on VHS.

The World is Never Blue Through Rose-Colored Glasses

Flowers are a bunch of pansies;
they only tell you what they think
you want to hear.

Never ask a flower a question
if a truthful answer is required.
You won't get it.
You can't count on flowers,
especially in important matters.

Loves me, loves me not?, you ask.
Loves you, loves you!, assures the flower.
So, should you go to him,
spill your heart in his lap
and flash your emotions in his face?

Heaven forbid!
You'll probably be arrested
for indecent exposure.

Betsy Mars
1986/May 2015

Rosé colored glass and the Blues

Changing purses I found the following evidence:
Two deactivated plastic hotel room keys.
Slightly crushed mints sentimentally saved for the next time
we'd be together. I believed.
A now rough-edged florist's card which had been attached to that bouquet sent
when I was having a bad day and
you still missed me. A rose petal pocketed somewhere between pages as
proof of love pressed.
A ticket to the art museum where we laughed
over my emotional likeness to Vincent Van Gogh
and your physical resemblance to that Wooden farmer granted.
A matchbook from the bar where we sat bartering and bantering:
my preferred beer in exchange for your favored oysters,
seeking common ground.
The beer clove-infused. The red oyster sauce piquant as we slip,
sliding away.
The blues played
out in that restaurant
where we had our last supper.
That night I still thought and fought and bought
your conviction that it would eventually be okay.
The next morning you called a taxi
which drove me away, like you,
still seen through rosé-colored glasses of wine
dulling the senses: a case of you
closed but for the lingering,
evidence of our failure and my unfailing
belief in flowers.

Sarah Thursday
2001/2015

Throat

I remember more than I want to admit
More than I can say out loud.
So much of it has never passed
through my vocal chords.
I can recall a picture at will.
I went so far as to type it out.
I can hold the pages in hand,
but I am afraid to see them.
Afraid to hear them read aloud.
It remains in my stomach,
where I stuffed it.
Sometimes it surges up like vomit
and I catch it in my throat.
It's like a rope pulled tighter.
My pain sits and I can not speak.
I am voiceless.
I find other things to talk about.
It settles back down.
I move on.
I have ulcers.

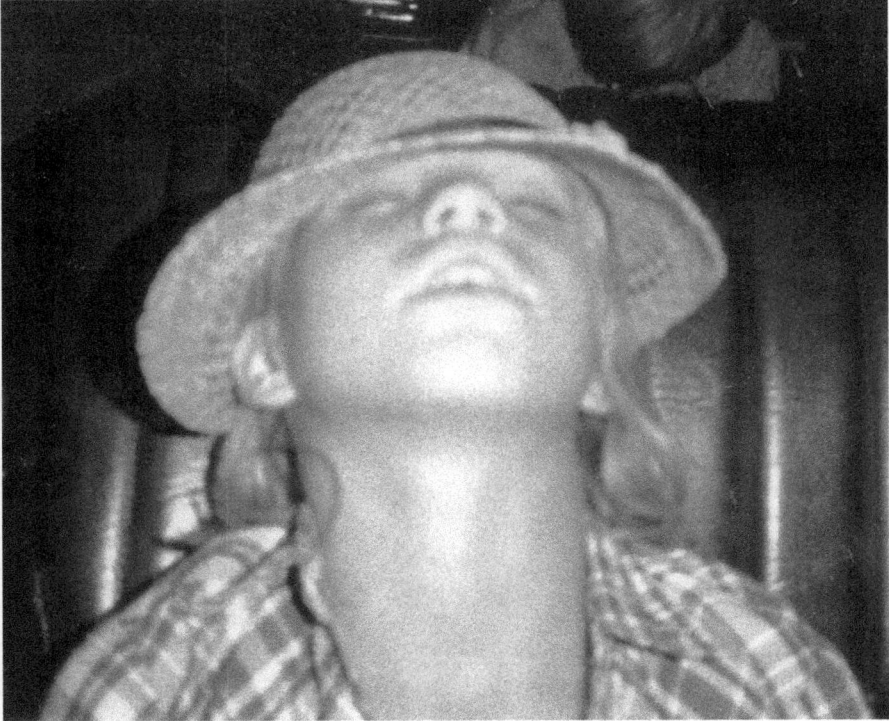

Tracheotomy

I said it all. Slit a line down my throat and pried it open like a dissected frog. I bent over and shook my head upside down to dump all that shit out. I don't have time for ulcers anymore so I cut a line through my esophagus, past my heart to my stomach. I used the sharpest knife I could find and scraped them out. Word after word corroding the stomach walls.   *daddy, sick, penis, bedroom, underwear*   My hands covered in black-tar memories. I scrape them all out.   *father, protect, shhhhh, coarse hairs, vagina*   I thrust the knife in deeper until I find the last of them.   *child, baby, girl, dim light, daddy*   I washed them all in the sink. I scrubbed, rinsed, and dried. Then set them in the full daylight sun. Some I kept, put them on the highest shelf. Others went one-by-one, slow and deliberate into a grinding disposal. The last of them rest safely between pages of poetry.

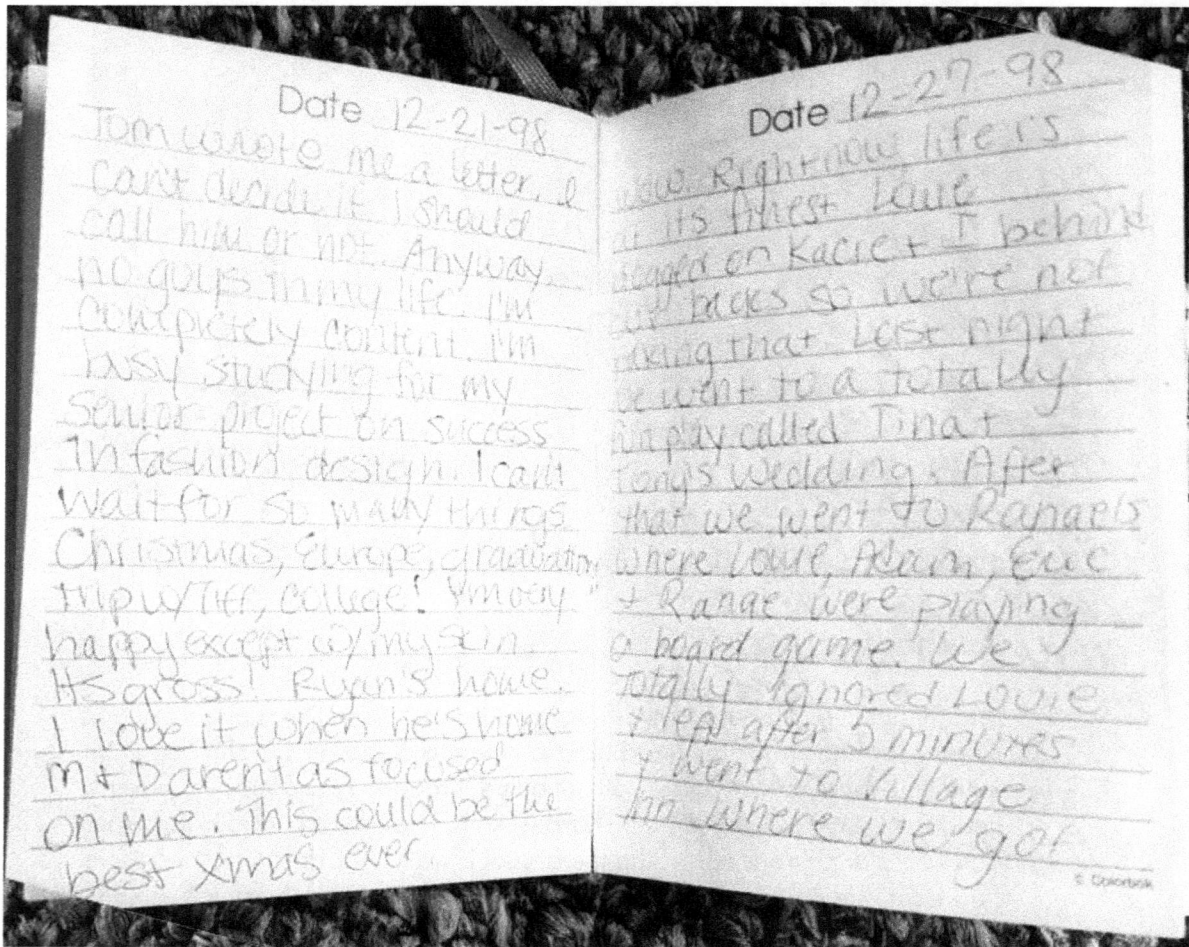

Sally Deskins
Diary, age 16/"Break the jar"

Twix Bars

You're a dirty little whore.
Did anyone ever tell you that?
Then I think it best for you
to hear it from me.
I have something to say to you,
And it's not very pleasant.
Get off my back you bitch.
Just leave me the hell alone.
Stop spreading needless rumors and gossip
And get a life of your own.
The two of you are over.
Face the facts.
You cheated on him.
I would never do that.
So I don't think you should be talking.
Great for you things didn't work out
between him and me.
Thanks to all your efforts.
Thanks to your jealousy and possessiveness.
Thanks for nothing whore. Now you
can go on obsessing without a threat in your way.

Laryssa Wirstiuk
2000/2015

Twix Bars

I promise to never call another woman
a whore, though I admit I've done it before.
Only now have I become sensitive to the word
"bitch" and won't even say it to my dog. More
than fifteen years later, my regret returns
to the cafeteria on a weekday after school
when we're waiting for buses, pressing faces
to vending machine glass. I purchase
a Twix bar, your snack of choice. Let's share
the man I wanted as my prom date and candy
I'd never normally eat. Pretzels and Diet Coke
were a treat only when consumed with delicious
rumors. Let's apply caramel to each other's lips.
Tell me why he bored you. I've seen the pictures
of you twice your age, betrothed, and one of him
in a dirty tie with his eyebrows set too far apart.
We're wearing the same blouse and plaid skirt,
and I suggest we choose dresses that instead
match our dreams: turquoise-bound islands
for you, urban paradises for me. Bound by
uniformity, I blamed my frustrations on a sweet
tooth who sugar-coated the lull of an afternoon.
I practiced words prohibited from academic
essays. You were less ideal and more context.

Crawl

Fitting but not fitting
Hard corners in lost patterns
There is a backside to
forever in the torn pieces
I have scattered.

I crawl until I walk
Among uncertain creatures
End of school days,
Avenues paved to
a new set of teachers.

Backside Of Forever

Then... I longed for freedom but
dreaded adulthood-spotlight on my face.
Tolerated the melt of simple days
that played like background

music at the circus.
I fought the prospect of
tugging weight of an obligated
life barefoot up the hill.

I burned as a lone birthday candle in
the cold gymnasium of Earth. Feared
being the most brave amoung sensible
cowards or first among all that failed.

Now I conjure the winds of today
I fan the heat of what can be.
I give a steady pressing motion
right at the very edge of me.

The next unlikely move, I claim
as my direction. I love All without
a backward glance into yesterday's
reflection.

G. Murray Thomas
1974/2015

Ace of Spades

Sits in the corner
quietly napping,
but watching the girls at play.
Fiddles with his fingers
under the table
then rolls his eyes away.
He watches intently
without moving a muscle
as the fingers turn slowly gray.
The sun slowly
on the staring eyeballs
still watching the girls at play.

Three of Clubs
(A self-portrait at seventeen)

Watching...
Always watching
Watching golden hair
        diamond eyes
        girls at play.
Not so much a stalker
        as a lurker
        (long before Facebook
        or even the internet).
A lurker in the physical world.
Always afraid
Afraid to approach
        to ask
        to act.
But also afraid
        I would grow old
without ever even moving.

A Life Unlived

Twenty years ago
she'd been engaged.
I'd like to think
she had a life,
and hopes and
dreams as young girls do.

I'd like to think
she'd made raucous love
on a pier in Monte Carlo

or tender love
beneath the cabin in which her
parents slept.

I'd like to think she'd kept her passport
in her purse
and bought lottery tickets.
And smiled into the eyes of strangers.

I'd like to think
it didn't used to matter
if there was no juice
or the refrigerator wasn't cold enough.

But I don't think that
would be true,
and seeing her today with nothing but
wearisome obligations
saddens me utterly,
for I have known her
twenty years
and have done nothing.

Maybe I have not watched a life unlived
but seen a destiny fulfilled.

Perhaps rigidness is in the bones
like an old dog with arthritis,
all dish towels folded equally
the toothpaste never squeezed.

Perhaps aloneness is in the soul.
When did she stop singing with the radio?

Tobi Alfier
October 2002/November 2009

A Life Unlived

Twenty years ago
she'd been bursting
with dreams of being famous
for her personality.
Twenty years ago
she'd made raucous love
on a pier in Monte Carlo,
kept her passport in her purse,
bought lottery tickets
and smiled into the eyes of strangers.

Twenty years ago
it didn't used to matter
if there was no juice
or the refrigerator wasn't cold enough.

When did she stop singing with the radio?

Alexis Rhone Fancher
Blonde Stealth/Blonde in Doorway #2

hauling ghosts

the loose antlers
dad lumbered
from garden to garden
transplant gingko
collection of succulents
(fat leaves i just want
to stuff into my mouth)
clowns
and then the other love
a wet cupped toad
grandma's night rhymes
blue nightgown murmurs
(bed company)
reclining her caves
skin's hold on
the knee's disaster
ghost's pale crowding
the blood out of heart
and right side
pumps empty

Kelsey Bryan-Zwick
2009/2014

hot lips' salvia and bougainvillea

sage lobs a grasshopper
hops larger than thought
wrought wings of strings
violins that jump immortal
sky, a hand out—

catch them, catches, them
eats them, stuffs them in jars
a twig, a leaf, opens
lets them go, jumps up
a butterfly, a drop of paint
petals a flutter

mother's flowers
on the counter, cut them
the stems, even, sink into
the vase, placed in the window
they are my eyes watching
outside, the hummingbird
drops down—still, flying
beneath the orange tree

grandpa's jade, I have seen
it so many places, like his ginkgo
both older than I am, the aloe
the yucca, the fountain my brother
dug up, the way he turns
the compost, for the first time

next to the blackberry vine
my mother nearly slaughters
every year, we search for
the berries—sweet, red candy

the treehouse decomposing
where we used to sit for hours
itchy with mosquito bites
trying to stay still
so spiders spin webs
in our hair, tangled—
in a nest of dress-up
clothes, magic beads
lantern full of dandelions

Mud Flowers

I buried you, Dad, at twelve
when my legs were shorter than your legs
and my feet rose only to your knees.
I piled the dirt heavy on your chest.
I watered your eyes,
drank your kiss
and sewed your encircling arms into sweaters.
She unwools them in the wind
and exposes her shoulders to leaves.
I smile. She smiles. We run.
This child doesn't carry coffins.
She follows them into the ground.
She likes her mud soft and her
carnations pressed cheek to cheek.
My carnations cough black pearls.
My father, your fingers fold over my face.
You draw dimples and plant wrinkles.
Pastel dresses don't fit anymore,
and braided hair ices my neck and chest.
But this night I'll climb your sands
and graze your seashells. Each one is a fossil.
Each one is a name. I've forgotten the names.
Now bottles sprout trees between rocks
and glass spiders coil my feet.

A piece of mirror spears my heel
and lodges there
for you, Dad, a winter home.

Petals in the Mud

I hear a child's laughter as I stand over
your grave where I left you all those years ago.
Mud seeps through my fingers
and fireflies flicker above us, elusive fairies
with their wings of broken light.

I want to turn back time and crawl
into your lap and show you my drawings.
I want so badly to forget.
If I hugged you again, would you be able
to hug me back, just a child and her father:
nothing more?

I don't want to open that door
and look in the room where we
all slept in one bed. I don't want you
to hold me like that, so close,
my nightgown a tangle in your legs.

It was much easier when I was twelve,
to bury you, to stroke your face in mud
and forget. I wanted to crawl into
your grave and let the petals cover both our faces,
let us sink into a bed of leaves.

Let your kiss be the wind, and memory the night,
my handsome, deadly father who drew the breath
from my chest with every brush of your lips.

Fernando Gallegos
"The Shadows" Then/Now

These Scars

Practitioners write me prescriptions for pills
which I gladly swallow to retain autonomy.
Without them, what life would I have?
chained to this earth, a mom and a dad?
These bastards tie oven mitts to our hands
tell us not to touch ourselves or each other.
Only in the abortion clinic will they finally
disclose the keys to your own body.
Men get all the fucking power.
A virgin never gets to be on top.
She's always beneath, receiving the thrust
of a man promising pleasure and love.
It goes without saying, he wears the condom.
And if it breaks, she'll pick up the pieces
wipe the semen off her hair
and get on with it.

The clock strikes twelve.
Feet begin to rot.
Have you ever bled during sex
because you were afraid to say "stop?"
The selfless giving of pleasure
I attempted to brainwash myself into enjoying
because, after climaxing,
he's so much easier to cuddle.
These gentle folds turn women into gods
and men into drooling babies.
I can't even cry, you expect me to orgasm?
In a position as vulnerable as a birthing mother?
The last man to eat me out wasn't a man.
It was a machine made to destroy unwanted zygotes.
Will your lips be that tender, darling?
Will you suck out all my worries, like it did?
Will you scar me for the rest of my life?
Do you take debit?

Your tongue brushes over the source of my misery.
My genital fluids are salty like tears.
I'm not turned on, darling, I'm crying.
My soul is deformed but my body is beautiful.
Give me a man to kiss these scars
and all they may hold.

The Trajectory of a Trauma

My mom said there were protesters
wielding hate signs and yelling about life.
She said I was pale as death
and nearly fainted in the humidity of the neon Tustin sun.

I don't remember any of that.

All I can remember now
is the anesthesiologist telling me to
count backwards from one hundred.
I stared up at silver stirrups
and somewhere around ninety,
reality slipped away.

All I can remember now
is waking up fully clothed
shivering in striped blue jeans
knowing I was bleeding from somewhere.

I try to remember more, but the memories
once haunting with lucidity
have slow-faded into sepia.
The trauma is a ship that set sail and sank
becoming just another forgotten death
covering the sea floor.

Kelsey Bryan-Zwick
Butterfly Pattern/Primavera

Amélie Frank
4/21/98 Old Lanscape/
6/23/2015 New Landscape

The Auk is Gone for Good

*"He could not, Himself, make a second self
To be His mate; as well have made Himself:
He would not make what He mislikes or slights,
An eyesore to Him, or not worth His pains"*
Robert Browning
Caliban Upon Setebos

A woman at work, 4-1/2 feet tall,
hairpin spine,
and a throw pillow for shoulders
Has anyone loved her? Ever?

My mother hunkers in the mud garden
trowel like a first tool, aggrieved with God
because she thinks she is someone's maid
Has my father loved her? Ever?

That is my bit of spine
in that bottle.
It is the missing link's wedding gift.
Will ensure fertility (ha-ha).
Tell me, do you think
I could have walked upright
if that little bone had
been in its proper place?
Would I have moved my opposable thumbs?
Invented the wheel?
Could I have aspired to beauty?
Successfully mated?
Have I a place in the fossil record?

This lizard moves through the world funny.
Easy for the cat to draw first blood.
The cat is not evil.
It is just in its nature
to snick a claw across
the lizard's spine.

That man is not evil.
It is just in his nature
to trap my bumbling form
in tar and stone
to exhibit my calcified heart
like an ugly bug
or a curiously paned leaf
like a bone in a bottle.

Keepsake. Conversation piece,
A slice of hip. The butt of a joke
I aspire to camouflage my strangeness
before that man makes like Ted Hughes
and burns the testimony and memory
—*that* evidence—
out of my flesh.

You see this, this ant in amber?
Ant aspires to glitter in the sun.
Beauty is an accident.
And my multitude of strangenesses
has no place in the George C. Page Museum

The Cicada Does Not Die in This One
(yet another poem for Peter Sharp)

She is the only one of the billions of her like
who can see the cooling of the new continent.
As she clings to the sprig of annexing kudzu
she mulls over the variables: the lull in the wind
the weakness in the new legs, the oil evaporating
from the clear, decorative lines that ushered in
the war to end all wars. These she understands
are the only assets, second to the awareness
that the wind is melting and the air thickens
with change. The others shall not hear
nor see nor taste it. The sea hisses
as the molten land finds its purchase

Steadying her perch on the sprig.
she hears the rising chorus of monkeys
the ones who remind her how very badly
she negotiated nymph-hood,
how transformation that comes so easily to
the multitudes didn't gel so well with her.
They chitter, "My shell will never harden!
That damned, stupid wing will not uncoil!
I will become snagged in my own casing.
I will never fly! And I will go unnoticed
because of these madcap, ladybug eyes!"

But elsewhere, the ocean seethes
and is not heard over the
wing-scrape Bacchanalia. Louder even
than the derision of the monkeys in her head
is the grind of the inexorable: the inaugural
strata; the unsuccessful handshakes between
seas of differing densities; the liquefaction of
the fossil registers; the poisoning of the well
of the great unconscious

Fate will be unkind to those who cannot change,
brutish to those who can see, but can do nothing.

She is not the only hobbled one.
Some dangle by a furled wing over eternity.
Some drop into the pond, cannot skip across water,
find themselves in the mouths of small fish
or devoured by turtles, ants, opossums.
Still, billions survive to find a mate.
She surveys her sisters and brothers in their
tipsy commute up the trees
It is mostly routine, the couplings,
the honeymoon hootenannies
the gaping and clasping of tail-ends,
and with that act, their lives are complete.
6 weeks above ground,
17 years under terra firma,
the casting forth of red-eyed and optimistic eggs.

And is she not changed in her maiden, mutant state?
Will she be black with red wings or green with blue wings
or turquoise all around? Will she be pretty?
Ultimately, she is amber fore and aft
a filter of the pre-dusk light,
nothing like the billions trundling off
to a happy sleep and crisp, dry deaths.

As the song goes, the wind blows some luck
in her direction. She plummets from the kudzu
and finds herself upswept into the thermals,
passage to the coagulating landform assured.
By the time she alights on whatever germinates there,
her destiny will pair with the antipodes
of her shed expectations. She has two things
going for her beside the amber wings:
courage and imagination, which meld to become
a budding knowledge that she was the very last
and will be the very first of her kind.

an untitled poem

do not ask me why i sleep
alone i feel to be a dream
and sometimes it's hard to
associate myself with my
illusions

yesterday was an older couple
    living beyond thin apart
ment walls throwing fists of
night at eachother yesterday
I could not sleep.   it makes no
difference

today is lying on a park bench
like a tired poor huddled mass
an undercover news paper man
watching the birds fly from limb
to limb

today i have been picking trees
and feeling the bouquet of eyes
as we nervously watch each
other and agree that we live
inside each

today has been spent walking on
the earth looking for to morrow   with
each the earth bends a little
more and i fear it's back
is breaking

this morning as you are sleeping
i am writing a poem to hand to you
and i will what i can
and i bring what i am
and all i am is what
i've found

Daniel McGinn
1975/2015

an untitled poem

do not ask me why i sleep
or why i wake
alone i feel to be a dream
a slow shifting shadow
and sometimes it's hard to
see a man i don't really
associate myself with my
rear view mirror
illusions anyway

yesterday was an older couple
with a couple of kids in tow
living beyond this apart
from meaning beyond those apart
meant walls throwing fists of
flowers from open hands into the
night at each other yesterday
i snuck up behind my family and
i could not sleep. it makes no
sense to ask you why or what
difference made us us anyway

today is lying on a park bench
soaking in a pool of sunlight
like a tired poor huddled mass
of ripples disappearing in heat
an undercover newspaper man
setting his notepads on fire
watching the birds fly from limb
floaters flapping burning hollow
embers drifting limb to limb

today i have been picking trees
to pepper with birdfeeder seed
and feeling the bouquet of eyes
hungry sparrows ogle me
and we nervously watch each
of the seeds i spill bounce, fall
and clump against each
other, we agree that we live
off what is given and held tight
inside each and every

today has been spent walking on
what's left of the old neighborhood
the earth looking for tomorrow with
sorrow and starvation blistering its feet
each step the earth bends a little
and bows to the hole in the sky once
more and i fear it's back
will never get better even though
we know it's breaking

this morning as you are sleeping
i pick up a pen and repeat myself
i am writing a poem to hand to you
a poem about home is where we live
and I will do what i can
to not be an idiot
and i will bring what i am
you will tell me i am worthy
and all i am is what
comes from love and what i love is you
i've found

Music Lessons

At ten, I was a perfectionist with bow ties.
My fingers were nimble then. My fingers were poised
for playing Beethoven with the symphony orchestra.

I missed baseball because the allegros took time.
I knew more about the language of musical time,
how if I held a note like a fair ball, people would applaud.

It was usually the sensitivity of the phrase
as my fingers lightly touched each note
like it was a hummingbird entering a flower.

I would stay up past midnight finding a stanza sobbing.
At times, I imagined reaching across the keys
like the distance between continents.

The girls barely noticed me; the boys mocked me.
I tugged at my loneliness like it was a neat bow tie.
Allegros took time reach the apex of each phrase.

It was the moment a flower accepted a hummingbird.
It was when continents shifted apart.
Each chord I memorized was a lost childhood.

Eventually, my ears lost perfect pitch.
The language of loss was fingered like flower petals.
The piano stopped searching for me.

My wife watches my fingers typing and notices
how they stretch across, playing the music of poetry,
making less sound than a hummingbird or tying a bow.

Martin Willitts Jr.
Past/Present

The Lesson

My younger brother broke my nose once just to hear the satisfying crunch. It sounded like dropping a lightbulb.

He would have hit me again, but I had stumbled away, staggering, leaving a trail of blood spore like a wounded eight point buck. He probably reflected upon what it would be like to use a ball peen hammer. He was always looking for the next level of pain.

He actually received praise from the doctor on the clean break. My parents suggested that I should learn how to duck. Someone said I should apply for a job as a punching bag. The doctor re-broke my nose in order to fix it. I was lights-out twice in one day. My nose was never quite right after this.

This broken nose lesson provided training for the unexpected. I learned that danger was everywhere; there was no safe place or quiet moment.

When he punched my nose hard enough to rattle my teeth, he bruised his knuckle. His girlfriend kissed his boo-boo; then accused me of harming my brother. When my brother found out that the doctor had broken my nose in order to re-set it and it was still messed up, he volunteered to hit it again.

After that my life was dodges, near-misses, on-going terror alerts. I reminded him I had once cleaned his diaper; he reminded me that he had once cleaned my clock.

Last year I found out my brother had cancer real bad. He was retching blood. I was flipping a coin: should I pray for his recovery; or, for his long painful death. When I saw how shaken and withdrawn he appeared, I began to pray.

Maybe those blows to my nose affected my judgment. Maybe I had learned no one deserves that much misery. Maybe in sixty years I had learned the right lessons.

Poet & Artist Bios

Tobi Alfier is a five-time Pushcart nominee and Best of the Net nominee. Current chapbooks are *The Coincidence of Castles* (Glass Lyre Press) and *Romance and Rust* (Blue Horse Press). Her collaborative full-length collection, *The Color of Forgiveness*, is available from Mojave River Press. She co-edits San Pedro River Review (www.sprreview.com).

Suzanne Allen has always written, but *Seventeen Magazine* never accepted any of her poems, perhaps rightly so. Now she is a Pushcart Prize nominee with poems published and anthologized in six countries and online. She co-edits *The Bastille*, (Paris, France,) and her chapbook, *Verisimilitude*, is available at CorruptPress.org.

Robin Steere Axworthy is a native Californian who wandered off for many years before returning home in 1983. She has been writing since childhood in the interstices of adulthood, marriage, child rearing, teaching, dancing, and etc. She writes poetry and fiction when she can.

Born in the Bronx, New York, **Judy Barrat**'s only credentials are her love of the written word. She has enjoyed writing poetry and fiction most of her life as a hobby in the hope of painting pictures with her words the way her grandfather did with a paintbrush.

Erica Brenes has a BA in Creative Writing from UCLA and a MA in English from CSULB. She teaches composition and literature at El Camino College and currently lives in Bixby Knolls with her husband. Her poetry and non-fiction essays can be found in *Cadence Collective*, *SAP*, *The Rip Rap*, and *Role Reboot*.

Kelsey Bryan-Zwick is a poet, a bookbinder, and an artist from Long Beach, California. She earned her B.A. in Literature/Creative Writing-Poetry from UCSC. Her new chapbook of poems and art, *Watermarked*, is now available from Sadie Girl Press.

Carla Carlson is a graduate of Sarah Lawrence College's MFA writing program. Her poems have appeared in *The Westchester Review*, *Fictionique*, *Chronogram Magazine*, *The Mom Egg*, *Catch and Release*, *Columbia Journal*, *Yes, Poetry*, and *Prelude Magazine*. Her first chapbook is being published by Finishing Line Press, to be released in 2015.

Marcus Clayton grew up in South Gate, CA, and holds an MFA in Poetry from CSU Long Beach. He is an editor for *American Mustard*, and an assistant poetry editor for *The Offing*. Some of his published work can be seen in *Tahoma Literary Review*, *Mason's Road*, and *Lipstick Party Magazine* among others.

Beverly M. Collins, is the author of the books, *Quiet Observations: Diary Thought, Whimsy and Rhyme,* and *Mud in Magic*. She is one of three prize winners for the California State Poetry Society 2012 yearly competition. She was born in Delaware and grew up in New Jersey.

Sally Deskins is an artist and writer focusing on women in art. Currently a graduate student at West Virginia University, she's been published internationally and exhibited nationally. She illustrated *Intimates and Fools* (2014, Les Femmes Folles Books) and *Leaves of Absence* (2015, Red Dashboard) both with poetry by Laura Madeline Wiseman. sallydeskins.tumblr.com

Brandon Dumais was born in LA and studied creative writing and English literature at CSULB. He is the co-editor of *Remedial Art Class* and currently lives in Indianapolis where he watches strangers' home videos for money. He understands the difference two years can make.

Born and raised in Seattle, living in Oakland, **Sharon Elliott** is a poet activist who has written since childhood. Four years in the Peace Corps in Nicaragua and Ecuador laid the foundation for her activism in multicultural women's issues. She loves cats, the sea and stormy days.

Alexis Rhone Fancher is the author of *How I Lost My Virginity To Michael Cohen and Other Heart Stab Poems*, and *State of Grace: The Joshua Elegies*. Nominated for three Pushcart
Prizes and four Best of The Net awards, Alexis is poetry editor of *Cultural Weekly* and photography editor of *Fine Linen Magazine*. www.alexisrhonefancher.com

Los Angeles native **Amélie Frank** is the author of five poetry collections. Her work has appeared in numerous local, national, and international publications. Co-founder of the Sacred Beverage Press, she produced the acclaimed magazine *Blue Satellite*. Her biography appears in *Who's Who in America* and *Who's Who of American Women*.

Fernando Gallegos is a Long Beach artist born and raised. He is heavily inspired by the human form and always searching to evoke the feeling of movement and emotion. Find more info and keep updated at FB\Fernando.Gallegos.LBC IG\@ fgraphix

John Guzlowski's writing appears in Garrison Keillor's *Writer's Almanac, North American Review*, and elsewhere. His poems about his parents' experiences as slave laborers in Germany appear in his book *Lightning and Ashes*. Of Guzlowski's writing, Czeslaw Milosz said, "He has an astonishing ability for grasping reality."

Robin Dawn Hudechek received her MFA in Creative Writing from UCI. Her poems have recently appeared in *Caliban Online, Silver Birch Press, Cadence Collective: Year 2 Anthology, Verse-Virtual, Chiron Review*, and *Poemeleon*. Robin lives in Laguna Beach, CA with her husband, Manny and two beautiful cats, Ashley and Misty.

Boris Salvador Ingles at his core bleeds Los Angeles. Born and raised in Boyle Heights. he finds beauty and soul in every disdain facet of life. Boris combines poetry and photography, as means for visual and emotional expression. A mixture of humor, rawness, vulnerability and a sense for dark street realism.

Brian Christopher Jaime has short stories & poetry published in several anthologies & publications including: *Embark to Madness, Dead Men and Women Walking: An Anthology of Things Undead, The San Gabriel Valley Tribune, & FlashShot*. He also made it to the top three of The New Camp Horror's 2004 Dark Idol competition. www.brianjaime.com

Ken Oddist Jones is a Long Beach graphic artist and photographer who studied at the Florida School of Art. His photography and digital collage varies from the carefree and whimsical, to the surreal and sometimes haunting. He's been featured in New Legends and at WE Labs' "Metamorphosis" show. Follow him on Facebook.

Frank Kearns was raised in New England. He is transformed into a Southern Californian by time in Venice, years at the Bethlehem Steel mill in Vernon, and a long career in the aerospace industry. He lives and writes with his wife Carol in Downey, California.

Avra Kouffman is a performance poet and writer who grew up in New York City and now lives in coastal California. She has taught writing at UC-Irvine and University of Arizona and facilitated writing workshops for New York Writers Coalition.

Sarah Lim, photographer and friend to the Bees, was born in the UK and raised in Tasmania, Australia. Sarah began photographing food creations in 2011 with a hand-me-down first generation iPhone. Since then photography has become a passion which she is delighted to share with her community. She is also a Farm to Table Chef!

Gerald Locklin is a Professor Emeritus of English from California State University, Long Beach, where he continues to enjoy the privilege of access to his old office and to teach when needed. He has published thousands of poems in periodicals and over a hundred volumes of poetry, fiction, and criticism. www.geraldlocklin.org.

Steven Marr, scientist, writer, and artist, is a second generation native of the Long Beach area. He studied at UC Santa Cruz and CSU, Long Beach holding degrees in Zoology and Fine Art. He has exhibited his art extensively at the community level and published one piece of his writing.

Betsy Mars is an educator, traveler, lover of animals and nature, proud mother of two adult children, and closet optimist and romantic. She finds it very gratifying when a poem emerges and tells her something about herself while also speaking to others. Betsy lives in Southern California and is very gradually sorting out her life.

Daniel McGinn's poems about his wife, his dog and the moon have appeared numerous anthologies and publications. Daniel has an MFA in writing from Vermont College of Fine Arts. He and his wife, poet Lori McGinn, are natives of Whittier, California.

Teresa Mei Chuc is the author of *Red Thread* and *Keeper of the Winds*. Her poetry appears or is forthcoming in *CONSEQUENCE Magazine*, *Kyoto Journal*, *Rattle*, *Whitefish Review* and in the anthologies *New Poets of the American West* and *Inheriting the War: Poetry and Prose by Descendants of Vietnam Veterans and Refugees*.

Natalie Morales has had dozens of her poems appear in publications such as Cornell University's *Rainy Day Literary Magazine*, *Pomona Valley Review*, and *Cadence Collective*, among many others. She currently attends a master's program at Cal Poly Pomona and continues to compile a her first chapbook.

Frank Mundo is the author of a novel-in-verse called *The Brubury Tales* (foreword by Carolyn See), a modern version of The Canterbury Tales set in Los Angeles just after the 1992 riots.

Brittni Suzanne Plavala is a poet from La Habra, CA, now living and loving in Sacramento. Since her memory began, her dreams have served as a catalyst for inspiration for many artistic mediums. Today, she studies Art History at CSUS and hopes to wrap up her first chapbook in 2016.

Joy Shannon is a visual artist, tattoo artist, performer, songwriter, writer and researcher. Perhaps best known for her Celtic pagan folk band Joy Shannon and the Beauty Marks, she is also a tattoo artist under the name Triple Goddess Tattoos. Shannon is currently writing a book of poetry and art to be released in the next year.

Clifton Snider is the internationally celebrated author of ten books of poetry, including *Moonman: New and Selected Poems* (2012), and four novels: *Loud Whisper*, *Bare Roots*, *Wrestling with Angels: A Tale of Two Brothers*, and *The Plymouth Papers* (2014). He has published hundreds of poems, fiction, reviews, and articles internationally.

Julie Standig, from New York, has studied at the Unterberg Poetry Center and participated in Writer's Voice. She has had poems published in *Alehouse Press*, *Arsenic Lobster* and *Covenant of the Generations*. She writes on trains, late at night and often somewhere between Long Island, Manhattan and Doylestown.

Kevin Patrick Sullivan's books include, *First Sight*, *The Space Between Things*, and *Under Such Brilliance*. His poems are in *Solo*, *Askew*, *Miramar*, *The Second Genesis*, and *Other Voices International*. He is the co-editor of the anthology *Corners of the Mouth A Celebration of Thirty Years at the Annual San Luis Obispo Poetry Festival*.

G. Murray Thomas used to stay up banging out poems on an old typewriter. Most of them were terrible. After moving to Southern California, he started getting the poetry thing down, and now has two books of poetry to his name: *Cows on the Freeway* (iUniverse 1999) and *My Kidney Just Arrived* (Tebot Bach 2010).

Lynne Thompson has authored two full-length collections of poetry: *Beg No Pardon* and *Start With A Small Guitar* as well as two chapbooks and an e-book. Recipient of a 2015 Fellowship Grant from the City of Los Angeles, she is Review & Essays Editor of *Spillway*.

K. Andrew Turner writes literary and speculative fiction, poetry, and nonfiction. He teaches and mentors creative writers near Los Angeles, where he lives, works, and writes in the San Gabriel Valley. He is the Editor-in-Chief of *East Jasmine Review* and a freelance editor. You can find more at his website: www.kandrewturner.com

Marco A. Vasquez received his MFA in Creative Writing at California State University, Long Beach. An award winning playwright, he is also the author of four books of poetry, one of which is part of Gary Soto's Chicano Chapbook Series. His first novel *Steven Isn't Normal*, was recently awarded an International Latino Book Award.

Esmeralda Villalobos is an artist from Guadalajara, Mexico, currently living in Southern California. Her primary media are oils and acrylics, but she also enjoys working in watercolors, ink, and other mixed media. Facebook.com/artworkbyesmeraldavg

Brandon Williams is a graduate of the University of California, Riverside. His work has recently appeared or is forthcoming in *Yellow Chair Review*, *Soundings Review*, *Huizache*, *Black Clock*, *CulturedVultures.com*, *Blue Earth Review*, *MIRAMAR*, *Connu*, and *Solo Novo*. A product of northern California, he finds himself constantly called back to the Sierra Nevada Gold Country.

Martin Willitts Jr. won the 2014 Broadsided award; 2014 Dylan Thomas International Poetry Contest. He has 11 full-length collections including forthcoming *How to Be Silent* (FutureCycle Press), *God Is Not Amused With What You Are Doing In Her Name* (Aldrich Press), and *Dylan Thomas and the Writer's Shed* (FutureCycle Press).

Laryssa Wirstiuk lives in Jersey City, NJ with her mini dachshund Charlotte Moo. Laryssa's collection of short stories *The Prescribed Burn* won Honorable Mention in the 21st Annual Writer's Digest Self-Published Book Awards. Her poetry, fiction, and creative nonfiction have been published in *Gargoyle Magazine*, *Word Riot*, *Barely South Review*, and *Up the Staircase Quarterly*. laryssawirstiuk.com

About the Editor

Sarah Thursday calls Long Beach, California, her home, where she advocates for local poets and poetry events. She runs a poetry website called CadenceCollective.net, co-hosts a monthly reading with G. Murray Thomas, and founded Sadie Girl Press as a way to help publish local and emerging poets. Her love of book layout and design began with her first chapbook where she taped her poems over photocopies of her favorite album covers and song lyrics. Twenty books later, her mission is to continue to incorporate poetry and art into online and print publications. Her first full-length poetry collection, *All the Tiny Anchors*, is available at SadieGirlPress. com.

Find and follow her to learn more on SarahThursday.com, Facebook, or Twitter.

(2015 photo by Alexis Rhone Fancher)

1989/2015

Thank You!

The editor would like to thank the following: First and foremost Terry Wright for her strong opinions and constant cheerleading, Raquel Reyes-Lopez for all her editorial assistance and encouragement, K. Andrew Turner for fantastic feedback and inspirations for the subtitle, and Alyssandra Nighswonger for coming through at the final hour. My loving family, especially my momma, Annie Freewriter. Again and again and again, the amazing poetic and artistic community that gives endlessly, even when given such a tough assignment! I am constantly humbled and in awe of all of you.

About the Assistant Editor

Terry Ann Wright recently received her master's degree from Goddard College, a progressive school that emphasizes community activism and democratic education. She has written and published poetry exclusively for the last fifteen years, receiving two nominations for the Pushcart Prize in the process. She spends her days ridding the world of comma splices, and nights planning food-based road trips and sometimes writing. Her poetry has appeared most recently in the journals *Carnival, East Jasmine Review,* and *Cadence Collective,* and the anthologies *Cadence Collective: Year One* and *Year Two; Gutters & Alleyways: Perspectives on Poverty and Struggle; The Language I was Broken In;* and *Like a Girl: Perspectives on Feminine Identity.*

(2015 photo by Robbie Brown)

1989/2015

About the Cover Artist

Alyssandra Nighswonger was born the Don Quixote of the Santa Ynez Valley, brought into the world in Solvang, amongst an assortment of windmills. Now, an artist and musician, her lance is her paint brush and her stallion, a guitar. Her present day windmill is to brush off the ordinary, and tell stories that bring joy. She hosts a weekly open mic night at the Viento y Agua Coffeehouse and hypnotizes crowds in Long Beach and surrounding areas with the kind of music that make you put down your beer and think about your mother.

Find and follow her at talesofalyssandra.com or Facebook.

(2015 photo by Lindseying Photography)

2007/2015

Acknowledgements

The following poems have been previously published in this or another form as follows:

Tobi Alfier's "A Life Unlived" (2009) in *Poetry Breakfast*

Kelsey Bryan-Zwick's "hauling ghosts in *Chinquapin Thirty* and "'hot lips' salvia and bougainvillea," in *A Poet Is A Poet, No Matter How Tall*

Sally Deskins' Teen self reflections collage (2015) in *Quail Bell Magazine*

Amélie Frank's "The Auk is Gone for Good" in *Poetry Superhighway*

John Guzlowski's "Cattle Train to Magdeburg" in *Lightning and Ashes*, Steel Toe Books, 2007

Robin Dawn Hudechek's "Mud Flowers" in *Ghost Walk*, 2015

Frank Kearns' "Words for Rain" in *Yearlings*, 2015

Sarah Lim in "SOL Kitchen Goddess" by Julie Monical

Gerald Locklin's "Route 36" in *Sunset Beach*, Hors Commerce Press, 1967 and "Thumbnail Guide for the Senior Couplers" in *Poets and Pleasure Seekers: New and Selected Poems, 2010-2015*, Spout Hill Press

Teresa Mei Chuc's "The Gambler" in *Mo' Joe Anthology*, Beatlick Press, 2014

Clifton Snider's "It Will Happen" in *Alchemy of Opposites*, Chiron Review Press, 2000

Kevin Patrick Sullivan's "Freedom" in *Bits and Pieces of Black on White*, DeeTree Press,1982

Sarah Thursday's "Throat" in *Healing the Heart of Ophelia*, 2001

Marco A. Vasquez's "Tripping Over My Machismo " in *Tripping Over My Machismo*, Bender Books

www.ingramcontent.com/pod-product-compliance
Lightning Source LLC
Chambersburg PA
CBHW081139090426
42736CB00018B/3411